Before We Forget

This work is dedicated to my mother, Maria Nicolaza Hernandez Cordero. Her boundless love, oral skills in Mexican history, and in poetry inspired this project.

Before We Forget

Maestra Ramirez

Technical Advisor – Anthony Partida

To order additional copies of this book, contact:
Xlibris
1-888-795-4274
www.Xlibris.com
Orders@Xlibris.com
789385

THE SACRED HISTORY AND MYTHOLOGY OF MEXICO THE AZTECS.

People of the Sun And the:

Huexotzincas, chalcas, Xochimilcas, cuitlahuacas, malinalcas, Tepanecas and matlacincas.

Known today as The Mexicans

THEIR HISTORY AND MYTHOLOGY
BY Maestra Ramirez
Technical Adviser Anthony Partida
Book one – Aztec Genisis
AN EDUCATIONAL SERIES FOR TEACHERS, PARENTS,
CHILDREN, AND THE INTERESTED WORLD POPULATION
Assorted and presented by a Retired Mexican
Teacher of Humanities, and the Spanish Language.
Certified to teach English as a second language
(TESL) for life by the State of California, USA.

INTRODUCTION

https://www.google.com/url?sa=i&rct=j&q=&esrc=s&source=im-ages&cd=&ved=2ahUKEwjy3_HN4JHgAhUoKXoKHW6F-CWoQjRx6BAgBEAU&url=https%3A%2F%2Fes.wikipedia.org%2Fwiki%2FArchivo%3ACodex_Mendoza_folio_7or_portion.jpg&psig=AOv-Vaw2x5ewEYWU4V6hYtr1vmujs&ust=1548808816453081

Codex Mendoza

The Tlacuilos were reporters of their time, they drew pictures in order to communicate to others and to make a record of their people. It is that thanks to them we know about Mexican history for they were at the side of Sahagun and many other early Mexican historians. For more information on Tlacuilos Codex Mendocino is a fascinating documentary.

Codices from before and after the Spanish invasion were / are made by Tlacuilos. Using deerskin or Amatl, a special bark of a special tree. Colors were taken from mother naturelike the Cochineal bug, which was used for red. Colors

were important for everyone since they came charged with meaning. Meaning was shared by the commoners and elite.

LANGUAGE

The Nahuatl language had been established as the Lingua Franca of the day, as English is for us today. PhD Terrence Kaufman, a renown linguist traces it along with speaking differences back to 500 CE. This date is an important point in history as we will continue to see in the fallowing books.

MEANINGS

Daniel G. Brinton, also an Americanist author interpreted and found an additional meaning to the Serpent;" woman of tweens". This, interpretation will be of significance and I will explore in future Aztec works.*

Mlinalli is an historical name along with others listed here. I will include in the 3rd or so book of this educational series right along with others listed above.

**Rig Veda Americanus by Daniel G. Brinton.*

Chicomostoc, the place of the seven caves, is situated In Aztlan, the place of whiteness. This is the birth of the People of the Sun before they made their 200- year sacred journey to the promised land. Other codices tell of the migration of the Aztecs such as codice term Aztec Chimalpopoca which is a copy of a perihepatic codice, but there are only a handful of them. The Aztecs are known by several names which is

explained by their conquests and so on. Baron Humboldt and other Americanist used the name Aztec as a generic form to refer to the Chichimec's; in this work I Will use the term in the following pages.

This plate shows the very start of the people's journey to the Promised Land. A sacred bundle, depicting dream-like distance. In Jungian view a dream-like state of mind is possible as it appears in the Collective Unconscious. Aztecs thought the minute bird was encouraging them to move out of the cave and interpreted the sounds as "Mexica Forward."

In addition, to Jungian view, then, we have that the cave is a symbol of motherhood and protection. While the cave is a symbol of motherhood, according to Eric Neumann most enclosures such as a house a school or even the inside of a cave remain potential symbols for motherly protection and a female's womb.

Water one of the most fundamental elements in human life is also present. It is a dualistic fact because it represents both life when born. However once born death must follow.

Eight nations are signified, on the left of the plate, by unique symbols. A sacred bundle is a wrapped collection of sacred items held by a carrier, shown on the right of the plate. According to some sources, sacred bundles are still used in Indigenous American ceremonial cultures.

Patricia Deveraux, a member of the Blackfoot Confederacy in Alberta, 'these are holy bundles given to us by the Creator to hold our people together ... They're the same as the relics from the Catholic Church. They are a demonstration of the holy spirit. They can heal people."

Aztec dancers in Mexico City begin their sacred dance with a ritual of similar meaning.

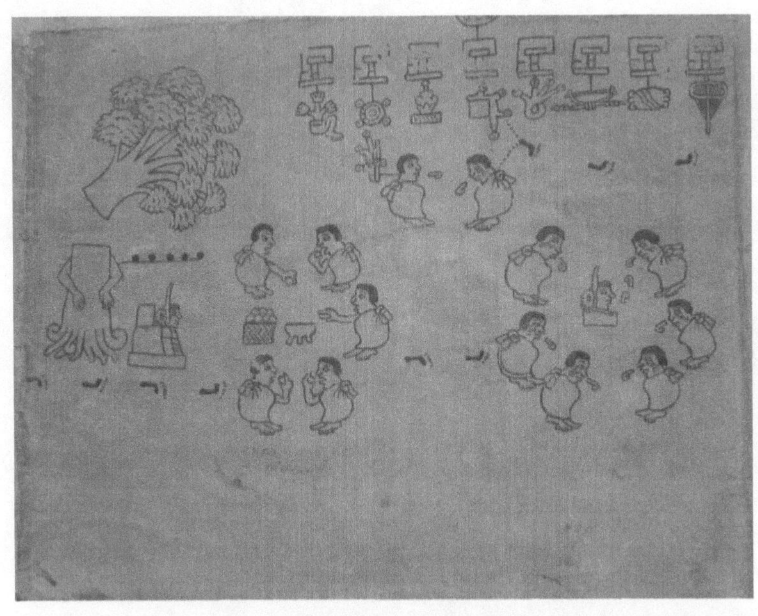

This plate shows the first time in which Aztecs sat down, rested, and communed. Huitzilopochtli, the Great Spirit gives two orders. One, they, from now on, they must identify as Chichimecas and not Aztecs. And, two, leave the other nations behind. Feeling deep sorrow everyone cried. From this time on, Aztecs continue their 200-year sacred journey in which they will continue to suffer badly. Survival will depend in much thought and strategy. But their main weapon of salvation was on the hands of the Great Spirit. Huitzilopochtli.

Intellectuals believe these were sacrifices prepared on Biznagas while commoners believed this was how they sent off their dead by cremation. .War, the pervasive human sentiment is present here.

Recently, Maria Castaneda de la Paz, investigator of the UNAM, recently provided additional insights to this complex mix media message.

This plate presents in Aztec numbers the sacred count they stayed in this particular place.

This plate shows a symbol of the sun carved in stone. The Aztecs had many different expressions to symbolize the sun. The sun is as we know today, a universal symbol to depict life and creation.

During the Renaissance in Italy, artist Rafael painted the creation of the Sun and the Moon by the creator, while Aztecs in Mexico were dancing to the same celestial manifestation.

The eagle in turn, is a symbol for the sun. The eagle is a predator of birds, snakes and more animals. The eagle is on the Mexican Flag but what it is eating has been the debate of many intellectuals. Thus, the varied versions of the eagle on the flag is a result of who/where and when the narrator first saw it. This image was selected for its majestic size and appearance at the doors of Templo Mayor in Mexico City- now a museum. Dr. Eduardo Matos Moctezuma standing next to the eagle statue. Archeologist and once director of the Museum of the city of Mexico.,

The Humming bird, a most admired bird for his extraordinary Feats by the Aztec. Have you ever seen one flying backward, upside down, or up and down? It reminds me of a Stealth plane or Harrier, but small, very small in size, but he was also a symbol of the sun.

Huitzilopochtli, the Sun, and the Creator, the main patron spirit of the people. According to sources he was the one who called them out of Chicomostoc to the promised land. The legend tells us that he was born from mother earth and when he was born, he was dressed up as a warrior. He told his mother not to fear the moon and the stars before he destroyed all of them. For they were unhappy with mother earth's behavior and wished to kill her.

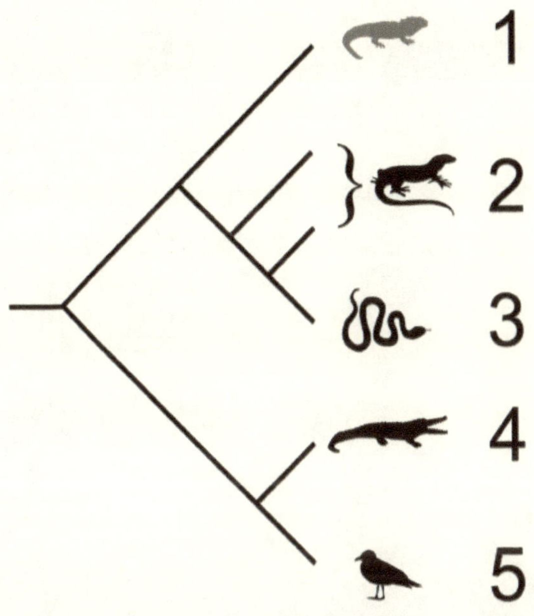

https://www.google.com/url?sa=i&rct=j&q=&esrc=s&source=images&cd=&cad=rja&uact=8&ved=2ahUKEwjGsqyNypjgAhXQJjQIHdj-4DOUQjRx6BAgBEAU&url=https%3A%2F%2Fcommons.wikimedia.org%2Fwiki%2FFile%3ATuatara_cladogram.svg&psig=AOvVawoFjb-pd7xjMy-QnYWt8l7km&ust=1549042949791719

Serpents and other reptiles are related to birds as depicted in this Reptile Family Tree.

The symbol on the pack of the first and second carrier is the serpent. The sacred bundle was also viewed as a medicinal bundle. This symbol is the winged serpent for modern people. Egypt had the first culture in recorded history that has the Serpent in its writings of religion.

This serpent symbol is one of its earliest Aztec representation. The serpent image is seen in many things throughout time including Modern Books such as "The Serpents Tongue" by Nancy Wood and many more.

THE PILGRIMAGE

Carriers were selected from amongst an elite and honorable people.

The first carrier named Tezcacoatl or mirror serpent. is the designated and chosen from an elite of knowledgeable people. He is carrying Huitzilopochtli. But the others, who belong to the same elite group of Teomamaque appear with a backpack ready to take and carry the sacred bundle. His name has a root connecting him to Tezcatlipoca.

The second carrier, by the name of Cihuacoatl, or Eagle serpent, together with the others leaving footprints behind, but no one knew for certain how long they would have to do this tortuous march. Again, the name has a root connecting him to the eagle.

The third carrier, by the name of Apanecatl or 'panache', such as the panache de-feather hair dress of Aztec ruler Moctezuma. His panache is currently located in Vienna Austria.

The forth carrier, by the name of Chimalma, was the only female carrier of the bundle. Chimalma is consort to Mixcoatl and future parents to Quetzalcoatl who was born in Teotihuacan.

The Milky was the symbol for Mixcoatl. His earlier manifestation comes as he is sitting outside the temple in front of Chimalma. It also appears to be the symbol that Chimalma carried on her pack.

This picture illustrates how long they stayed next to water on their way to the Promised Land.

This plate illustrates the point in which the people continued being mercenaries of war and the last plate in the Codice Boturini

LEANING OBJECTIVE

My objective partially draws its substance from modern and ancient, poetry, religion, science, psychology, and linguistics of the world. For this purpose, I have selected Mexican text material from best sources possible; archeologists and historians and other fields of knowledge as well.

Decidedly few Mexicans are aware of the rich legacy our American ancestors left for us. The world on the other hand interested in Aztec culture more than often are afraid of learning from miss informants. Any insights I have given are based on these teachings. In this hands-on work, you will be able to teach or learn from your own selection. Special links herewith included intended to be of some help.

SPECIAL SOURCES
Smith Michael E. Arizona State University
"Aztec culture flourished in the highlands of central Mexico between the twelfth and sixteen centuries, AD. Writes Dr. Michael E. Smith, Arizona State university in his essay AZTEC CULTURE: AN OVERVIEW (2006) p. 1, 2, and 3:

ORIGIN AND DEVELOPMENT

"...The early Aztec peoples were divided into a number of different ethnic groups. each located in its own region of central Mexico.

. .... also included the Acolhua of Texcoco the Tepanecas of Azcapotzalco ...the chalcas, Xochimilcas, Tlahuica and Tlaxcalteca.

These Aztec ethnic groups all spoke Nahuatl ...culture that was expressed in religious, economic, social, and political institutions and practices.

RELIGION

Aztec religion was polytheistic, but deities did not exist as discrete... gods and goddesses were seen more as forces of spirits..."

NOTES

STUDENT'S DRAWINGS